We need to try to i
to have put such fa
badly wrong. We n
of complete empt
appears that every
ready to receive t
beginning, which is

C000293423

This new beginning is found in an empty tomb. Those angels who appear to the women, telling them not to be afraid, deliver the starting point for all that follows: 'You are looking for Jesus of Nazareth who was crucified,' they say. 'He has been raised; he is not here' (Mark 16.6).

Not recognised ...

In St John's account Mary Magdalene goes to the tomb on her own. When she finds the stone rolled away and the tomb empty, she runs and fetches Peter and John. They go into the tomb and we are told that John 'sees and believes' (John 20.8). But what he sees is emptiness. He has not yet seen the Risen Lord.

Mary then lingers at the tomb and sees someone she mistakes for the gardener. He asks why she is crying and what she is looking for. Still convinced that the body has been taken, she asks if he knows where it might be. It is only when he utters her name that she recognises him as Jesus.

This initial lack of recognition is the next important piece of the puzzle. (And remember, the two disciples on the Emmaus Road didn't recognise the Risen Jesus either.) The tomb is empty because Jesus is now alive with a new and different sort of life. This new risen life flows from, and is continuous with, the life he had before. He has not become a different person.

So Mary Magdalene is not looking at a ghost. His risen life is still a *physical* life. In later resurrection stories, Jesus eats with his disciples. Thomas is even invited to touch the wounds where the nails had been.

But neither is Mary looking at a resuscitated corpse. Jesus has not been raised in the same way that Lazarus was raised, only to die again. Mary Magdalene is now looking at (and holding on to) the 'first fruits' of the new creation – the new heaven and new earth of which the whole narrative of Scripture speaks. Jesus goes before us to prepare a way. And on the first Easter morning he stands in our midst, showing us what our future will be.

So it is that Mary Magdalene becomes the first witness to the resurrection. She bears the message of the resurrection to the other disciples. Hence she is sometimes referred to as 'the apostle to the apostles'.

He is Risen!

So this is the first precious gift in the legacy of Jesus – those things that he left behind. *An empty tomb.* And the message from the empty tomb is the central message of the Christian faith. He is Risen! There is now a new hope and the promise of a new life for the whole of God's beloved and broken humanity.

Of course it is baffling. Of course it is unexpected. It confounds the wisdom of the wise and the piety of the religious. You can't pin it down. ('Do not cling to me,' says Jesus to Mary Magdalene [John 20.17]. I don't live in boxes. I jump out of tombs!)

There is evidence, though you can't prove that it happened. Yet without Jesus' resurrection, the Christian faith makes no sense at all. And, as we shall see, if it never happened, it gets progressively harder to understand why the followers of Jesus went on to do all the other things they did.

The resurrection is the hard, non-negotiable starting point of everything we know as Christian. This man Jesus, who died upon the cross and was buried in the tomb, is now *alive*. He has left the grave behind, and he has changed for ever the way we feel about death. More than this, we can now understand his own death: not as a failure, not only as an execution – but as the offering of his own life to God. He was indeed God's Messiah. But not in the way anyone was expecting.

As John the Baptist said of Jesus, 'Look, there is the Lamb of God who takes away the sin of the world' (John 1.29).

The resurrection of Jesus Christ is clearly an amazing event. It is also a highly *significant* event. In the New Testament, Jesus' resurrection is described as the 'first fruits' of a great harvest. *We* are that harvest. To change the image: Jesus threw wide open the gates of glory. The poet John Donne, Dean of St Paul's from 1621 to 1631, caught this in his sonnet *Death be not proud*:

Death be not proud, though some have called thee
Mighty and dreadful, for, thou art not so ...
One short sleep past, we wake eternally,
And death shall be no more. Death, thou shalt die.

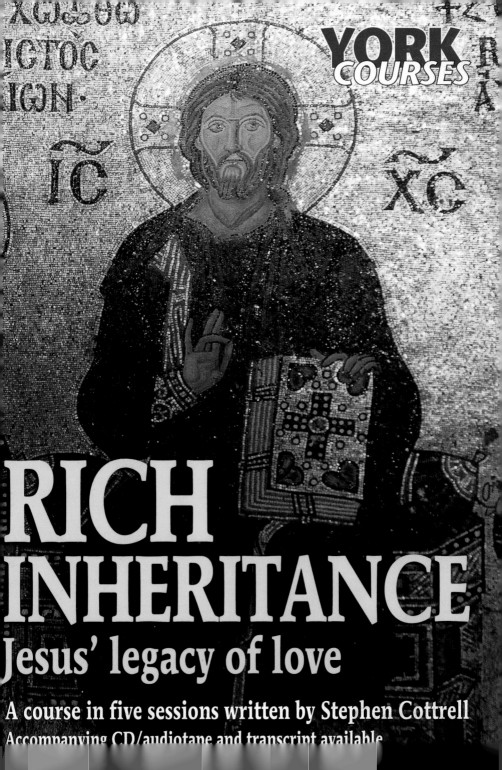

YORK
COURSES

RICH INHERITANCE
Jesus' legacy of love

A course in five sessions written by Stephen Cottrell

Accompanying CD/audiotape and transcript available

- *York Courses* are designed for groups and individuals. They consist of a course booklet, CD or audiotape, and transcript. The CDs/audiotapes feature distinguished contributors from a wide range of churches and traditions. This makes the material ideal for ecumenical use. Many groups use the material during Lent, but the courses can be used at any time of year.

- Details of our courses and publications are listed in the centre pages of this booklet. Fuller details of our range, including the latest special offers and discounts, are available at www.yorkcourses.co.uk where you can order securely online.

- To enable each group member to have their own personal copy of this booklet, the price is reduced either when multiple copies are ordered or if you order online at www.yorkcourses.co.uk

DETAILS OF PARTICIPANTS

on the CD/audiotape may be found on the inside of the back cover of this booklet.

COPYRIGHT:

PHOTOS:

Front cover image:
Mosaic detail from Hagia Sophia, Turkey.
Photographer: Suat Eman
www.freedigitalphotos.net

Page 6 - Empty tomb by McIninch*

Page 15 - Mystery Plays by Elaine Stanley

Page 18 - Bread and wine by Ingrid HS*

* www.bigstockphoto.com

Designed and printed by The Max Design & Print co. York

Rich Inheritance is about Jesus' legacy – what he bequeathed to the Church and the world, in order that the good news he came to bring might be heard and experienced by all. This booklet has been written by Bishop Stephen Cottrell. I'm a great admirer of his unique style of addressing complex issues with down-to-earth humour and plain common sense. I wish you every blessing as you gather together to explore the riches of Jesus' everlasting inheritance.

Dr David Hope
Archbishop of York
1995-2005

OUR WARM THANKS to Mark Comer of *The Max Design & Print co.* for his invaluable help and expertise. Thanks also to Yolande Clarke and Linda Norman for proof reading; to Katrina Lamb who prepared the Transcript; and to *Media Mill* for recording and producing the audio material.

THE COURSE TRANSCRIPT provides a complete record of the 'conversation' between the presenter and participants on the CD/audiotape. In an easy-to-follow format, the transcript booklet cross-references with the track numbers on the CD – making it simple to find the start of each new question posed to the participants. The transcript is especially useful for group leaders as they prepare. It can also help group members feel more confident about joining in the discussion – and enables them to go over the recorded material at leisure.

SUGGESTIONS FOR GROUP LEADERS

1. **THE ROOM** Discourage people from sitting outside or behind the main circle – all need to be equally involved.

2. **HOSPITALITY** Tea or coffee on arrival can be helpful at the first meeting. Perhaps at the end too, to encourage people to talk informally. Some groups might be more ambitious, taking it in turns to bring a dessert to start the evening (even in Lent, hospitality is OK!) with coffee at the end.

3. **THE START** If group members don't know each other well, some kind of 'icebreaker' might be helpful. For example, you might invite people to share something quite secular (where they grew up, holidays, hobbies, etc.). Place a time limit on this exercise.

4. **PREPARING THE GROUP** Take the group into your confidence, e.g. 'I've never done this before', or 'I've led lots of groups and each one has contained surprises'. Sharing vulnerability is designed to encourage all members to see the success of the group as their responsibility. Ask those who know that they talk easily to ration their contributions, and encourage the reticent to speak at least once or twice – however briefly. Explain that there are no 'right' answers and that among friends it is fine to say things that you are not sure about – to express half-formed ideas. However, if individuals choose to say nothing, that's all right too.

5. **THE MATERIAL** Encourage members to read next time's session *before* the meeting. It helps enormously if each group member has their own personal copy of this booklet (so the price is reduced either when multiple copies are ordered or if you order online). *There is no need to consider all the questions.* A lively exchange of views is what matters, so be selective. You can always spread a session over two or more meetings, if you run out of time!

   For some questions you might start with a few minutes' silence to make jottings. Or you might ask members to talk in sub-groups of two or three, before sharing with the whole group.

6. **PREPARATION** Decide beforehand whether to distribute (or ask people to bring) paper, pencils, hymn books, etc. If possible, ask people in advance to read a Bible passage or lead in prayer, so that they can prepare.

7. **TIMING** Try to start on time and make sure you stick fairly closely to your stated finishing time.

8. **USING THE CD/AUDIOTAPE** Some groups will play the 14-minute piece at the beginning of the meeting. Other groups will prefer to play it at the end – or to play 7/8 minutes at the beginning and the rest halfway through the meeting. The track markers (on the CD only) will help you find any section very easily, including the Closing Reflections, which you may wish to play again at the end of the session. You can ignore these markers altogether, of course, if you prefer.

SESSION 1

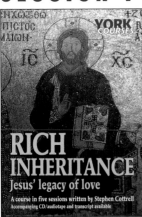

RICH INHERITANCE
Jesus' legacy of love

A course in five sessions written by Stephen Cottrell
Accompanying CD/audiotape and transcript available

AN EMPTY TOMB

> The divergences [in the Gospel accounts of the resurrection] appear very great on first sight ... But the fact remains that all of them, without exception, can be made to fall into place in a single orderly and coherent narrative without the smallest contradiction or difficulty beyond a trifling effort to *imagine* the natural behaviour of a bunch of startled people running about in the dawnlight between Jerusalem and the Garden.
>
> *Dorothy L Sayers, author and playwright*

Introduction

Jesus didn't write a will. He left no written instructions. He didn't seem to have a plan. At the end, as he hung dying on the cross, almost all of his followers had abandoned him. By most worldly estimates, his ministry was a failure. All that he left behind was a group of people – and most of them were illiterate peasant fishermen. It was not the most promising of starts!

Nevertheless, he charged them with responsibility for taking his message of reconciliation with God to the whole of the world. How did they do it? What else did Jesus leave behind that changed them, and made what happened next possible?

To begin at the beginning

Try to imagine what it would be like to hear the story of Jesus for the first time. His death on the cross seems like a terrible defeat; his resurrection an astonishing surprise. That is what it was like for the first followers of Jesus.

They didn't know what was going to happen next. When Mary Magdalene and the other women went to the tomb on that first Easter morning, they weren't expecting to find anything other than a corpse. As far as they were concerned, it was all over. Jesus was dead. Their hopes had been in vain and that was the end of it.

And even when they do discover that the tomb is empty, they don't immediately conclude that Jesus is risen from the dead. Resurrection was as strange and bewildering to people then as it is to us now. It was not something that people believed in or expected. Nevertheless, although the four Gospels offer different accounts of what happened on that first Easter morning, they are united about this: *the tomb was empty*.

In each of the Gospels, the resurrection itself – or at least the absence of Jesus' body from the tomb – was greeted with fear. The women were absolutely petrified. The stone in front of the tomb had been removed. The guards were gone. The body of Jesus was missing, presumably stolen. All they knew was that something terrible had happened. But they didn't think it was a resurrection. That's why the angels at the tomb greeted them by saying, 'Don't be afraid.' And that's why Jesus said, 'Peace be with you.'

So in order to make sense of what happens next, and to understand how the Church came into being – then grew and flourished – we need to make this our starting point.

QUESTIONS FOR GROUPS

BIBLE READING: John 20.1-18

Some groups will address all the questions. That's fine. Others prefer to select just a few and spend longer on each. That's fine too. Horses for (York) Courses!

1. **Re-read John 20.10-11** and the Archbishop Worlock box on p. 4. Imagine Mary Magdalene's deep sadness on visiting the tomb on that first Easter morning. If you've experienced times of desolation in your life, you might share them with the group.

2. **Re-read John 20.16-17.** In a short time Mary's desolation turned to joy. What has brought joy into your life during the past year or two?

3. **Read 1 Corinthians 15.20.** The empty tomb speaks of wonderful truths – resurrection and new life in heaven. Discuss the words of Archbishop Desmond Tutu and Sr Wendy Beckett in the box on p. 4 – and any of the other quotations which intrigue (or infuriate!) you.

4. The disciples look for Jesus in the tomb, but it is empty. A 'lapsed' friend tells you they want to 'find God again' and reconnect with their faith. They look to you for advice. What would you say?

5. **Read 1 Peter 3.15.** A sceptical friend asks how you, an intelligent person, can possibly believe the Easter story. How would you respond?

6. **Read 1 Corinthians 15.54-56** and the John Donne lines (opposite). Do you ever consider your own death and have you made any preparations for it? Does 'the hope of heaven' have practical implications for you as you live your life, and as you ponder your own mortality?

7. **Read Matthew 28.20b.** The New Testament claims that Jesus is alive and active in our world and in our lives. What does Jesus' promise: 'I am with you always' mean to members of your group? Does it make a practical impact on your lives?

8. **Read Matthew 28.19-20.** One key Christian calling was given first to Mary Magdalene: 'Go and tell'. If the flame of faith is not handed on, it will die. How can you do this as a church, as a group, and as an individual?

9. Read the Tom Wright box on p. 3. How do you keep Easter as a church, as a group, as an individual? Are you content with this, or does Bishop Tom have a point?

10. Listen again to track [5] on the course CD – or read the transcript. Archbishop Vincent Nichols speaks of 'the abiding presence of Christ' in the Eucharist and in the body of Christ. In your experience, is God always to be found in the 'expected' places – Holy Communion, the Bible, Christian fellowship ...? Paula Gooder talks of God appearing in *un*expected places. What might this mean? Can group members illustrate from personal experience?

11. **Read Matthew 8.23-27.** Jesus rebuked his disciples for their lack of faith: 'O ye of little faith'. Yet on the course CD [track 11] Archbishop Vincent Nichols says that doubt is part of discipleship. And Jim Wallis wants to distinguish doubt from disbelief. Drawing on your own experience, what do you make of these statements?

12. In his Closing Reflection on the CD [track 12] Inderjit Bhogal says: 'Liturgy can't cope with silence.' Do we use too many words in church? If so, how can we get a better balance?

'... the place where God's great truth is manifest: that love is stronger than death' (Canon Giles Fraser).

'No resurrection; no Christianity.' So said the great Archbishop Michael Ramsey. By which he meant that if God had not raised Jesus to new life, there would be no New Testament. We would have no record of Jesus' matchless teaching in the Gospels, there would be no great cathedrals, no Handel's *Messiah*, no Leonardo's *Last Supper* – and probably no hospices. The empty tomb inspired all this, and launched the biggest movement in history. This is how one man sees it:

For me, no other subject can rival its scale and drama. For 2,000 years Christianity has been one of the great players in world history, inspiring faith, but also squalid politics. It is an epic story, starring a cast of extraordinary people, from Jesus himself and the first apostles, to empresses, kings and popes; to reformers and champions of human conscience; to crusaders and sadists. Religious belief can transform us for good or ill. It has brought human beings to acts of criminal folly as well as the highest achievements of goodness and creativity.

Professor Diarmaid MacCulloch on BBC TV; author of *A History of Christianity*

SESSION 2

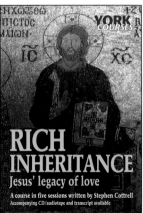

YORK COURSE

RICH INHERITANCE
Jesus' legacy of love

A course in five sessions written by Stephen Cottrell
Accompanying CD/audiotape and transcript available

A GROUP OF PEOPLE

On that first Easter Day Jesus met with a small group of people. They were his disciples: a motley band of dreamers and schemers. Several of them were uneducated peasant fishermen; one was a former tax collector. They didn't fit the profile for the sort of people we might expect to be chosen for such a great task. But it was through *these* people that God's message of reconciling love was going to be made known to the whole world.

They had followed him on the road throughout the three years of his earthly ministry, but they had rarely understood what he was talking about. They had liked it when he performed great signs, and when the people flocked to him. They had found it much more difficult when he shunned the crowds, or taught in his bewildering riddles. And when he seemed to court controversy and deliberately rile the authorities, they got very nervous. It had all become too much for them. They didn't dare admit it, but some of them were probably relieved it was all over.

How could it be otherwise? They were neither ready for nor aware of the task that lay ahead. They didn't 'get it' when Jesus was teaching them on the road. And they don't 'get it' even now, when Mary Magdalene tells her strange tale of an empty tomb and a risen Lord. It doesn't make any sense to them. They lock themselves away, frightened that they too might be arrested and crucified.

Jesus appears in their midst. He explains the Scriptures to them, helping them to see that it was necessary for the Messiah to suffer and to die. It was only through suffering that God could show real solidarity with the terrible suffering of the world. And it was only through dying that he could be that 'Lamb of God, who takes away the sin of the world' (John 1.29) – a perfect offering, perfectly made.

That is it. Yes, he does give his disciples his Spirit, and this obviously makes a profound difference. But it doesn't change the fact that, to carry forward God's mission of love, Jesus first forms a community of very ordinary men and women. He entrusts them with the task. Then he leaves.

Again, the different Gospels give differing accounts. But it all adds up to the same thing. In Matthew's Gospel Jesus tells them to go into all the world and make disciples (Matthew 28.19). He then ascends into heaven. In John's Gospel, on the first Easter Day, he says: 'As the Father had sent me so I am sending you' (John 20.21).

A new vicar wanted to pass the peace on the first Sunday in his new parish. As he approached one woman, she backed away. On leaving church she did shake his hand, so he asked why she'd refused to do so earlier. 'Vicar,' she said, fixing him with a straight look. 'I come to Church to worship God – not to be friendly.'

7

Gathered in ...

This community of very ordinary men and women still exists today: it is called the Church. In fact the word 'church' means 'gathered'. We are the people who have been gathered together by Jesus. We exist, not because of our goodness, or brilliance, or holiness, but because we have – in one way or another – encountered the risen Jesus.

We try to be good and we try to be holy. *But what matters most is our response to Jesus. And that his life and message should be communicated through us.* This is expressed in many different ways, depending on denomination, church tradition and culture. But in all our different manifestations we are still the same community. We are *the Jesus people* – centred on him who centres his life on us.

... sent out

We start as a gathered community. But that is not where it ends. Those first disciples – those who followed Jesus – are also called 'apostles' (which means 'those who are sent'). It is the same for us today. We are gathered for a purpose: to receive and enjoy the grace of God that is given to us through Jesus. Then we are sent out – to share God's love with our hurting and divided world.

The Church is therefore the 'gathered in' *and* the 'sent out' community of God. The task that was given to those first disciples is also given to us. We are the disciples/apostles of Jesus *today*. It is *our* job to make known the death and resurrection of Jesus. It is *our* calling to live by the standards of that new creation, and by the new humanity that we have seen in him. It is *our* challenge to live according to the values of the Kingdom of God – to try to live the way Jesus lived.

A new commandment

To help us do this, Jesus also leaves behind some uncomfortably revolutionary suggestions. He says that we must love one another. He says that we must love one another 'as I have loved you' (John 13.34) – that is, with the same committed, self-forgetful love with which he loves us. He calls this the 'new commandment' and he gives it to his friends on the very night of his arrest. Jesus demonstrates this by washing their feet and says that they must do the same for each other – and for everyone else too.

He says that they must love their enemies as well as their friends. And he says that they must carry on abiding in his love, making their home in him.

In other words, even though you are an *apostle* (one who is sent out), you never stop being a *disciple* (one who is gathered in) too. This is the rhythm of the Christian life. We come to Jesus within the community of his Church to learn from him and to enjoy his presence. We are sent out by him to serve the world.

And the really hard truth is this: whether we like it or not, most people today will judge the Church, and evaluate the meaning and value of the gospel, on the evidence of *our* lives. Once people know that we go to church, they will look at us to see if church makes any difference.

Down the centuries the Church has often failed miserably to live this radical way of love. But when it does – and when people catch glimpses of this way of life – then miracles happen. People and communities are reconciled. Despair gives way to hope. New possibilities for peaceful and equitable living are opened up.

To this day, some of the greatest good that is done across our world is still inspired by that way of life lived perfectly by Jesus, and entrusted to his Church.

The body of Christ

Jesus describes his followers as 'salt and light' (Matthew 5.13-16). St Paul describes the Church as Christ's 'body' (Romans 12.4-8). Christ is the head, and we are the limbs and organs. Each one of us is an essential part, inter-connected with the whole and with a particular job to do.

QUESTIONS FOR GROUPS

BIBLE READING: John 20.19-23

1. **Re-read John 20.19.** Think of the first disciples waiting nervously in the upper room. Then think of a time in your own life when you were really nervous about tackling a difficult task or facing an uncertain future. Share experiences.

2. **Re-read John 20.19.** Imagine that you are one of the disciples in the upper room on that first Easter Day. Outline the conversation which you took part in before Jesus appeared.

3. **Read Hebrews 12.1.** From the earliest days some individuals from 'the group' (i.e. the Church) have inspired others. Describe one or two people you have known, or heard about, who inspire you in your Christian faith and seem to show you Jesus by the way they live?

4. In your experience, what is the best thing about being a follower of Jesus? And what is the toughest?

5. **Read Mark 1.16-18.** A young person says, 'I want to be a disciple of Jesus. How do I begin? What does following Jesus in the 21st century involve?' How would you answer?

6. **Read Matthew 28.16-20.** How might you/how do you – as an individual Christian and as a member of your church – fulfil your 'apostolic calling' to share the gospel in your neighbourhood?

7. **Read Romans 12.1-8** and re-read the final paragraph of this session (p. 9). What do you think Jesus meant by 'salt and light'? What is your particular 'job', do you think? Check with other group members to see if they think you've got it right.

8. **Read Micah 6.6-8.** Listen again to track [14] on the course CD (or read the transcript). Jim Wallis suggests that faith in God should be *personal* but not *private* – and that it must sometimes be *political* (e.g. opposing racism). How does your own faith square up to this? Group members are invited to share their insights.

9. **Read Hebrews 10.23-25.** Archbishop Vincent Nichols [track 17] talks about the importance of re-connecting with people who have left (often just drifted away from) church. Can you think of people who have drifted away? Have you ever done so yourself? If so, why? And what brought you back?

10. **Read Luke 15.1-10.** How does/how might your church attempt to reconnect with people who have left? An increasing number of churches are observing 'Back to church Sunday' each Autumn. And some churches produce invitation cards for members to give to friends for special Sundays such as Harvest Festival, Mothering Sunday or St Valentine's Sunday. Might these ideas work in your congregation? Can you make other suggestions?

11. Select two or three quotations from the boxes in the margins which you would like to discuss.

12. Raise any points from the course booklet or CD/audiotape which haven't been covered by your group, but which you would like to discuss.

SESSION 3

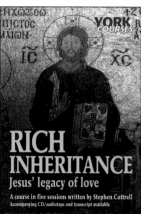

RRICH INHERITANCE
Jesus' legacy of love
A course in five sessions written by Stephen Cottrell
Accompanying CD/audiotape and transcript available

A STORY

I wasn't brought up as a regular churchgoer. I first encountered the real impact of the Christian story when I saw the television film *Jesus of Nazareth* when I was about fourteen. I can still remember the power of the story – especially the crucifixion. For the first time its meaning and relevance burnt its way into my heart.

It had such a powerful impact that I found myself weeping uncontrollably. Those were the days when there was only one television in most homes and watching programmes was a family activity. Embarrassed by this show of emotion, I remember running from the room and throwing myself onto my bed.

After a little while my mother came into the room to see what the matter was. She comforted me, but after a while she also, nicely, told me to pull myself together. The trouble is, I couldn't. I couldn't then, and I can't now. The power of this story changes lives. So it is that the Christian *faith* is first and foremost the Christian *story*.

So what did those first Christians *do* when Jesus sent them out to conquer the world with his message of love? Well, yes, they did marvellous things in the power of God's Spirit – and we will look at these in the next session. But most of all they *told a story*.

- *They told* people what God had done in Jesus.
- *They explained* the difference this had made in their own lives.
- *They declared* that it could make a difference for the whole world.

On the day of Pentecost – the day the Church received the Holy Spirit – St Peter gets up and preaches his very first sermon. (It was quite a bit shorter than some of the sermons you hear today, and that is no bad thing!) At its heart Peter simply tells people of the things that he has seen and experienced.

He tells the crowds that they have crucified the One who was sent by God, and that God has vindicated him by raising him to new life. He tells them of the impact that Jesus has had on his own life. (Peter can't pull himself together either!) Later on the authorities expressly forbid Peter from teaching in the name of Jesus. He responds: 'We cannot keep from speaking about what we have seen and heard' (Acts 4.20).

A city of two tales

Peter is telling *two* stories. He is telling people about Jesus. And he is telling people about his personal

---

It takes a thousand voices to tell a single story.
Native American saying

The destiny of the world is determined less by the battles that are lost and won than by the stories it loves and believes in.
Harold Goddard

The gospel is first and foremost not a message that is declared, nor a strategy that is launched, but a life that is lived.
Robin Gamble

experience as a follower of Jesus. Two thousand years later the stories are not so closely interwoven for us as they were for Peter, but, essentially, we are called to do the same thing. Like Peter then, Christians today have two stories to tell:

- We tell the story of what God has done in Jesus.
- We tell the story of what God has done in us.

Both stories are important. Both are precious.

The work of communicating God's Kingdom, and the new humanity he has created in Jesus, involves the telling of both stories.

People need to know the story of Jesus. It is a tragedy that many young people are growing up in our country without knowing even the basic facts about his life and ministry. After all, you cannot really understand the culture in which we live – its art and music and literature – without knowing something about the faith that inspired it. The work of Christian witness must always point to Jesus, for it is through Jesus that God tells the story of his love.

Paradoxically, it is often the telling of our own story which is the best way into telling the story of Jesus.

We live in challenging times. Some people are suspicious of all claims to universal truth. Many are cynical about anyone who offers optimism and hope. Many still cling to a so-called rational and scientific world view that they fancifully imagine has somehow 'disproved God'. Consequently, the whimsical speculations of Dan Brown and the intemperate put-downs of Richard Dawkins seem to get a better airing than the gospel of Jesus Christ. (And by the way, the most up-to-date historical, archaeological and critical assessments of the New Testament lead us to have even greater confidence that these are historical documents that get us very, very close to the person of Jesus himself.)

What people *will* listen to is the testimony of others – the stories we tell about our own experience. Personal experience is something that cannot be gainsaid or disproved. We may not like it; we may not agree with it – but we cannot simply dismiss it.

You may think that Science has disproved God, or that the New Testament is unreliable. But you cannot dismiss the heartfelt experience and living testimony of a friend who simply tells you what faith means for them. This is how the gospel spread in the first place (and we can read about it in that actually very reliable book called the Bible!).

YORK COURSES

'Spiritually profound [and] illuminating'
Professor Basil Mitchell, University of Oxford

These three...
FAITH, HOPE and LOVE

FIVE SESSIONS: Believing and trusting; The Peace of God; Faith into Love; The Greatest of these; All shall be well

Based on the three great qualities celebrated in 1 Corinthians 13. This famous passage begins and ends in majestic prose. But the middle paragraph is practical and demanding. St Paul's thirteen verses take us to the heart of what it means to be a Christian.

with **Bishop Tom Wright, Anne Atkins, The Abbot of Worth. Professor Frances Young.** *Introduced by* **Dr David Hope**

THE LORD'S PRAYER
praying it, meaning it, living it

FIVE SESSIONS: Our Father; Thy will be done; Our daily bread; As we forgive; In heaven

In the Lord's Prayer Jesus gives us a pattern for living as his disciples. This famous prayer also raises vital questions for today's world in which 'daily bread' is uncertain for billions and a refusal to 'forgive those who trespass against us' escalates violence.

with **Canon Margaret Sentamu, Bishop Kenneth Stevenson, Dr David Wilkinson.** *Closing Reflections by* **Dr Elaine Storkey.** *Introduced by* **Dr David Hope**

CAN WE BUILD A BETTER WORLD?

FIVE SESSIONS: Slavery – then and now; Friendship & Prayer – then and now; Change & Struggle – then and now; The Bible – then and now; Redemption & Restitution – then and now

We live in a divided and hurting world and with a burning question. As Christians in the 21st century how can we – together with others of good will – build a better world? Important material for important issues.

with **Archbishop John Sentamu, Wendy Craig, Leslie Griffiths. Five Poor Clares from BBC TV's The Convent.** *Introduced by* **Dr David Hope**

WHERE IS GOD...?

FIVE SESSIONS: Where is God when we .. seek happiness? ... face suffering? ... mak decisions? ... contemplate death? ... try to mak sense of life?

If we are to find honest answers to these bi questions we need to undertake some seriou and open thinking. Where better to do this tha with trusted friends in a study group around thi course?

with **Archbishop Rowan Williams, Patricia Routledge** CBE, **Joel Edwards, Dr Pauline Webb.** *Introduced by* **Dr David Hope**

BETTER TOGETHER?

FIVE SESSIONS: Family Relationships; Churc Relationships; Relating to Strangers; Broke Relationships; Our Relationship with God

All about relationships – in the church an within family and society; building stron relationships and coping with broken ones *Better Together?* looks frankly at how th Christian perspective may differ from that o society at large.

with **the Abbot of Ampleforth, John Bell, Nicky Gumbel, Jane Williams.** *Introduced by* **Dr David Hope**

TOUGH TALK
Hard Sayings of Jesus

FIVE SESSIONS: Shrinking and Growing Giving and Using; Praying and Forgiving; Lovin and Telling; Trusting and Entering

Looks at many of the hard sayings of Jesus in th Bible and faces them squarely. His uncomfort able words need to be faced if we are to allow th full impact of the gospel on our lives. *Tough Tal* is not for the faint-hearted.

with **Bishop Tom Wright, Steve Chalke, Fr Gerard Hughes SJ, Professor Frances Young.** *Introduced by* **Dr David Hope**

NEW WORLD, OLD FAITH

FIVE SESSIONS: Brave New World?; Environment and Ethics; Church and Family in Crisis?; One World – Many Faiths; Spirituality and Superstition

How does Christian faith continue to shed light on a range of issues in our changing world, including change itself? This course helps us make sense of our faith in God in today's world.

with **Archbishop Rowan Williams, David Coffey, Joel Edwards, Revd Dr John Polkinghorne KBE FRS, Dr Pauline Webb.** *Introduced by* **Dr David Hope**

IN THE WILDERNESS

FIVE SESSIONS: Jesus, Satan and the angels; The Wilderness Today; The Church in the Wilderness; Prayer, Meditation and Scripture; Solitude, Friendship and Fellowship

Like Jesus, we all have wilderness experiences. What are we to make of these challenges and how are we to meet them? *In the Wilderness* explores these issues for our world, for the church, and at a personal level.

with **Cardinal Cormac Murphy-O'Connor, Archbishop David Hope, Revd Dr Rob Frost, Roy Jenkins, Dr Elaine Storkey**

FAITH IN THE FIRE

FIVE SESSIONS: Faith facing Facts; Faith facing Doubt; Faith facing Disaster; Faith fuelling Prayer; Faith fuelling Action

When things are going well our faith may remain untroubled, but what if doubt or disaster strike? Those who struggle with faith will find they are not alone.

with **Archbishop David Hope, Rabbi Lionel Blue, Steve Chalke, Revd Dr Leslie Griffiths, Ann Widdecombe MP**

JESUS REDISCOVERED

FIVE SESSIONS: Jesus' Life and Teaching; Following Jesus; Jesus: Saviour of the World; Jesus is Lord; Jesus and the Church

Re-discovering who Jesus was, what he taught, and what that means for his followers today. Several believers share what Jesus means to them.

with **Paul Boateng MP, Dr Lavinia Byrne, Joel Edwards, Bishop Tom Wright, Archbishop David Hope**

LIVE YOUR FAITH

SIX SESSIONS: The Key - Jesus; Prayer; The Community - the Church; The Dynamic - the Holy Spirit; The Bible; The Outcome - Service & Witness

Christianity isn't just about what we believe: it's about how we live. A course suitable for everyone; particularly good for enquirers and those in the early stages of their faith.

with **Revd Dr Donald English, Lord Tonypandy, Fiona & Roy Castle**

GREAT EVENTS, DEEP MEANINGS

SIX SESSIONS: Christmas; Ash Wednesday; Palm Sunday; Good Friday; Easter; Pentecost

Explains clearly what the feasts and fasts are about and challenges us to respond spiritually and practically. There are even a couple of quizzes to get stuck into!

with **Revd Dr John Polkinghorne KBE FRS, Gordon Wilson, Bishop David Konstant, Fiona Castle, Dame Cicely Saunders, Archbishop David Hope**

2 ADDITIONAL COURSES

ATTENDING, EXPLORING, ENGAGING

with **Archbishop David Hope, Steve Chalke, Fr Gerard Hughes SJ, Professor Frances Young**

FIVE SESSIONS: Attending to God; Attending to One Another; Exploring Our Faith; Engaging with the World in Service; Engaging with the World in Evangelism

THE TEACHING OF JESUS

with **Steve Chalke, Professor James Dunn, Dr Pauline Webb, Archbishop David Hope**

FIVE SESSIONS: Forgiveness; God; Money; Heaven and Hell; On Being Human

Comprising photocopyable notes, audiotape and photocopyable transcript

AUDIOTAPE: £8.99 *(£6.99 each for 5 or more)*
TRANSCRIPT: £4.99
PHOTOCOPYABLE NOTES: £3.10

CD CONVERSATIONS

ROWAN REVEALED

The Archbishop of Canterbury talks frankly to Canon John Young of *York Courses* about his life and faith, prayer, poetry, the press, politics (including the war in Iraq), the future of the Church, 'fresh expressions', what Jesus means to him ...

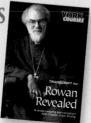

 ## SCIENCE AND CHRISTIAN FAITH

An in-depth discussion with the Revd Dr John Polkinghorne KBE FRS, former Professor of Mathematical Physics at Cambridge University.

CLIMATE CHANGE AND CHRISTIAN FAITH

Nobel Prize winner Sir John Houghton CBE, FRS is a world expert on global warming, its implications and remedies. He talks on this CD about "Why I believe in Climate Change" and "Why I believe in Jesus Christ".

PRAYER

Archbishop David Hope on *Prayer*. Four Christians on praying ... for healing; in danger; in tongues; with perseverance.

This CD accompanies the booklet *The Archbishop's School of Prayer*

1 CD	**£5.00**
Multipack of **5** identical CDs	**£10.00**
Multipack of **25** identical CDs	**£25.00**
Rowan Revealed transcript	**£2.99**

TOPIC TAPES

 ## STRUGGLING/COPING

4 personal conversations – £5 each tape

TAPE 1: *Living with ... depression; ... panic attacks*
TAPE 2: *Living with ... cancer; ... bereavement*

(Both tapes for £8.50)

FINDING FAITH £1.99

is a 20-minute audiotape, designed for enquirers and church members. Four brief stories by people, including Archbishop David Hope, who have found faith.

Inexpensive! Designed as a 'give away'

BOOKLETS and BOOKS

ARCHBISHOP'S SCHOOL SERIES

7 BOOKLETS COMMISSIONED BY Dr DAVID HOPE – Prayer; Bible Reading; Evangelism; The Sacraments; Christianity and Science; Healing and Wholeness; Life After Death.

99p
each

Authors include John Polkinghorne and David Winter

Special offer: Complete set of all 7 booklets only £5

CHRISTIANITY – AN INTRODUCTION

Fully revised in 2010

Hodder paperback, written by John Young, author of most of our course booklets.

£10.99

And this is how faith spreads today – once we begin to get the story out. First of all our story of who God is for us – then the central story: that of Jesus himself.

A story not a statement

It is also wise for us to remember that the Christian faith was a set of stories before it was a set of statements. This is because there are different sorts of truth. There's the truth that can be demonstrated objectively – facts like size and weight. Then there's the truth about a human relationship, in every respect a deeper and more important truth, though it's not something that can be easily measured or verified.

The truth about God is like this. And what God offers and desires is *relationship*. That is why in Jesus he sends us a *man* not a *manifesto*.

A beautiful truth

The truth about God is multi-faceted, like a beautiful jewel. Most of us will only ever see or appreciate a small part of it. Like every relationship, there will always be more to learn. But this also means that our story – our small glimpse of the multi-faceted truth – is precious and important, not just for us but for others. We will see and experience something of the beauty and majesty of God that others are not seeing and not experiencing. Therefore it is all the more important that we learn how to share it. Jesus left us this treasure, not just for the evangelisation of the world, but in order to build up and fill in our picture of who God is – so that our understanding of the glory of God might grow.

Jesus the storyteller

When Jesus opened his mouth to teach, it was usually a story that came out. He knew this was the best way to communicate the sorts of truths that couldn't easily be pinned down: the sorts of truths you had to learn, inhabit and embody for yourself. Our holy book, our Bible, is in actual fact a library – a collection of books, which are themselves collections of stories. Inspired by the Spirit of God, they don't provide easy answers. But they are a gateway into our relationship with God, so that we can become part of the story.

13

QUESTIONS FOR GROUPS

BIBLE READING: Acts 4.1-22

1. *Read Matthew 13.44-46.* What is your favourite parable or miracle of Jesus? Why do you particularly like it?

2. You meet a Buddhist who asks you to outline the story of Jesus in the Bible. Rehearse your answers now!

3. *Re-read* the first three paragraphs of Session 3. Paula Gooder [track 28 of the CD] suggests that Christians are often reluctant to talk about their journey into faith, experience of God, or the impact faith makes on their lives. Invite group members to share their own stories right now – whether dramatic or not!

4. Would you like to hear personal experiences in church – interviews with people, perhaps – instead of sermons, from time to time?

5. *Read Matthew 7.28-29.* What is it about the story of Jesus that most attracts you – or puzzles you? Jot down two or three things, before sharing them with the whole group?

6. *Read Acts 8.26-38.* Have you learnt most about God and the Christian life from sermons, books, other people, prayer, directly from the Bible – or in some other way? Can you think of a particular sermon, book, conversation, action ... which changed the way you came to think about God and your life?

7. *Read Acts 16.6-10.* Can you point to an experience when you felt that God was working in, or influencing, your life in some way? If so, is this a regular or a rare occurrence for you?

8. *Read Deuteronomy 6.4-9.* On the CD [track 30] Simon Stanley says, 'the Bible stories, once so familiar, are now largely unknown and untaught. Many people think this is a disaster'. Do you agree? And if so, what can we do about it?

9. Surveys suggest that even many churchgoers do not read the Bible. Does this matter? Is this a hindrance to our personal Christian development (our 'walk with God') – or can we learn about Christian faith and life in other equally helpful ways?

10. All our participants on the CD agree that 'stories are vital'. Do you find dramatic stories – along the lines of Jim Wallis's amazing anecdote [track 23 on CD] – encouraging, inspiring, or perhaps 'off the wall'?

11. *Read Matthew 28.19-20.* 'The story and gospel of Jesus is a precious gift we have to share' (Inderjit Bhogal on the CD). Yes, but how can we do this in our culture which is often not eager to hear?

12. Select two or three quotations from the boxes in the margins which you would like to discuss.

13. Raise any points from the course booklet or CD/audiotape which haven't been covered by your group, but which you would like to discuss.

The scriptures are the scrapbook of the Judeo-Christian family: our treasured repository of the stories and shared memories that make us who we are. Out from its hallowed and well-thumbed pages tumble not just the official line but all the little asides and keepsakes that remind us of the colourful and roguish characters we have in our family history, and the incredible story of our journey.

Dean Richard Giles

The medieval cycle of York Mystery Plays in 2010. 'The greatest story ever told' has been enacted since the Middle Ages.

SESSION 4

RICH INHERITANCE
Jesus' legacy of love
A course in five sessions written by Stephen Cottrell
Accompanying CD/audiotape and transcript available

A POWER

On the night before he died, Jesus said something rather strange to his friends. He said, 'It is to your advantage that I go away, for if I do not go away, the Advocate will not come to you; but if I go, I will send him to you' (John 16.7).

Jesus is speaking about the Holy Spirit. A little earlier he had said: 'The Holy Spirit will teach you everything, and remind you of all I have said' (John 14.26). And further on he says: 'When the Spirit of truth comes, he will guide you into all truth' (John 16.13).

The word 'advocate' is one of several words used in English Bibles to translate the fairly untranslatable Greek word *paraclete*, which in turn is one of John's words for the Holy Spirit. It is a legal term which refers to someone who speaks on behalf of another. But sometimes *paraclete* is translated as 'comforter', suggesting one who cares for and supports another.

Jesus is making two crucial points:

- the Holy Spirit could not come until he departed. He is referring to his ascension into heaven – the event recorded at the end of two Gospels (Matthew and Luke) when the resurrection appearances come to a close and Jesus ascends to the Father.
- the Holy Spirit will be an active – though 'un-pindownable' – power in their lives.

God's Spirit will remind his disciples of old truths and lead them into new ones. He will defend and challenge, comfort and cajole. Above all – and this is what the disciples can't really understand yet – the Holy Spirit is the *Spirit of Jesus*. So the Spirit cannot be given until Jesus has departed. And Jesus cannot depart until his mission is complete.

Therefore, Jesus' ascension should not be seen in terms of *absence*, but of *presence*; not *departure* but *arrival*. The ascension is the completion of God's reconciling work in Christ. Jesus arrives to be with God – and it is 'the man Christ Jesus' (1 Timothy 2.5) who sits at the Father's right hand.

In Jesus it is human flesh and blood that is glorified and honoured in heaven. Christ's sacrifice is complete. In a wonderful 'exchange', the Holy Spirit arrives on earth so that the presence of Jesus is no longer limited by time and space. Through his Spirit, Jesus can give himself both equally and immediately to all believers – including us. It is through the power of this outpouring that the mission of God's Church really begins.

The gift of the Spirit

The New Testament offers us two contrasting stories of this climactic event. Each has something important to tell us.

In John's Gospel it happens on Easter Day itself. Jesus says, 'As the Father sent me, so do I send you' (John 20.21). On hearing these words of commission, the disciples must, initially, have felt completely overwhelmed. It was hard enough for them to come to terms with Jesus' presence with them – now he was asking them to share that presence with everyone else! How could they possibly do this?

Well, the answer is – by the power of the Holy Spirit.

In the Fourth Gospel, the frightened and confused disciples are given the Spirit there and then. They stand in the upper room, wondering how on earth they are to fulfil the mission God has given them. Then Jesus breathes upon them, saying, 'Receive the Holy Spirit' (John 20.22).

According to John, the gift of the Spirit is closely bound up with the giving of authority to continue the ministry of Jesus: 'If you forgive anyone's sins,' says Jesus, 'they are forgiven' (John 20.23).

In Luke's Gospel, the disciples are told: 'Wait in the city until you have been clothed with power from on high' (Luke 24.49). Then the actual giving of the Spirit comes early on the Feast of Pentecost. This is recorded in the Acts of the Apostles (Acts 2.1-13). In Luke's account the Spirit is about continuing the ministry of Jesus: the disciples speak in many different languages; the word of God can now be heard in all the world.

The fruit of the Spirit

There is a wild unpredictability to the Spirit. Like the Risen Christ himself, God's Spirit cannot be pinned down. That's why there are so many different images for depicting the Spirit – a dove at Jesus' baptism; water at our own; wind and fire on the day of Pentecost; breath to the disciples in the upper room. But the consistent teaching of the New Testament is that the Spirit will be known by *the fruit produced in human lives*.

In his letter to the Galatians (5.22-23) Paul lists this fruit as 'love, joy, peace, patience, kindness, generosity, faithfulness, gentleness and self control'. But I don't

---

It is often in groups of Christians meeting for prayer that a new openness to the Spirit is discovered. It is in such groups that it is vividly realised that the prayer of Christians is not of their own strength or initiative; the Spirit prays within them and they participate in the Spirit's prayer.

Archbishop Michael Ramsey

The Christian Church... did not begin with a new doctrine or theory. It began with a remembrance of the life, death and resurrection of Jesus, and with the wind and fire of God, sweeping through human lives and changing them forever.

Professor Keith Ward

Love is a fruit in season at all times and within the reach of every hand.

Mother Teresa of Calcutta

The Spirit ... was a *fact of experience* in the lives of the earliest Christians.

Professor James Dunn

The Holy Spirit may without exaggeration be called the heartbeat of the Christian, the lifeblood of the Christian Church.

The Church of England's Doctrine Commission

believe this list is intended to be exhaustive. The Holy Spirit is the Spirit of Jesus – manifesting himself in different ways, in different people, at different times. As Paul goes on, 'If we live by the Spirit, let us also be guided by the Spirit' (Galatians 5.25).

This will mean being led into new truths and towards new challenges. And in every situation that we face, the Spirit will be fruitful in our lives in new ways.

The gifts of the Spirit

A good tree bears good fruit. Over time the fruit of the Spirit grows from the ceaseless activity of the Holy Spirit in our lives. Paul encourages the more 'dramatic' gifts of the Spirit, such as prophecy and speaking in tongues (1 Corinthians 14.1-5). But he insists that whatever languages we speak – human or divine – the greatest gifts will always be faith, hope and love (1 Corinthians 13.13). Once again we see that these manifestations of the Spirit are manifestations of Jesus himself.

The Spirit in the Church today

Jesus bequeaths his Spirit to his Church. The Spirit is the gift that unlocks and animates all other gifts. Without the Holy Spirit there could be no Church and no mission.

But it is vitally important to realise that the same Holy Spirit is just as available to us today as in those first heady days of Christian mission. The Spirit of Jesus is not a finite resource. It's not as if Jesus gave such a huge dose of the Spirit to his disciples then that there's not much left for us now!

We may not be very ready to receive the Spirit – or expectant of what he can do in our lives. But the Spirit still wants to

- make Jesus known
- grow beautiful fruit in our lives

And God the Father still wants to

- pour his Spirit onto his Church
- pour a Spirit-filled Church into the world.

For it is only by the Spirit of Jesus that we can witness to the resurrection of Jesus; it is only by the Spirit of Jesus that we are formed as his body; and it is only by the Spirit of Jesus that we are enabled to tell his story.

> Our message ought to be the power of the risen Christ. If we live in that power, why should we worry? How can we ever lose?
>
> *Canon Giles Fraser*

We receive this Spirit in baptism – and we can receive the Spirit afresh each and every day. It is the Spirit who propels and shapes the Church, its teaching, its ministry and its sacraments. As we shall see in the final session, it is the Spirit that comes down upon the bread and wine at Holy Communion, so that in sharing them with one other we receive the risen life of Christ, and are nourished for our ministry in the world.

The New Testament makes a distinction between the *fruit* of the Spirit and the *gifts* of the Spirit. God wants to grow every single one of the fruits of the Spirit in every life. In contrast, the gifts of the Spirit are spread throughout the Church. The Greek word is *dollops* – one here, two there ... but never none. In this way God ensures that the Church works as an organism, called the body of Christ (1 Corinthians 12.12-30). The Catholic theologian Karl Rahner is helpful here: *The gifts of the Spirit are never all given to one individual. They may – like healing powers or speaking in tongues – be quite extraordinary and even spectacular in nature. But they can also be almost secular, everyday capabilities, up to the point of good cash administration of a parish or community.*

On the CD Archbishop Vincent Nichols links the Holy Spirit (Session 4) with Holy Communion (Session 5).

QUESTIONS FOR GROUPS

BIBLE READING: Ezekiel 37.1-6

1. **Read Hebrews 3.13.** Discussing the gifts of the Spirit on the course CD [track 40] Paula Gooder speaks about the importance of *encouragement*. Describe people who have encouraged you in your life and with your faith.

2. **Read John 14.16 and 14.26.** In the New Testament the Holy Spirit is given many names, including 'Comforter' or 'Counsellor'. On track [35] of the course CD our participants discuss this title. Share with your group an occasion when your faith brought comfort or direction into your life, perhaps during difficult times.

3. **Read Ephesians 4.1-6.** In the Bible the Holy Spirit brings unity and harmony [discussed on track 36 on CD]. Do these qualities characterise your church – and relationships between churches in your locality? Which areas need developing – and how might you do this?

4. **Read Galatians 5.22-23.** The Spirit's work in human lives is often gentle. As a group exercise help each other commit to memory the nine qualities listed by St Paul as 'the fruit of the Spirit'.

5. Reflect on your own life. Which of these 'fruits' of the Spirit feature strongly in your life, and which need greater development in your view? Share with the group. Invite their comments if you dare!

6. **Read 1 Corinthians 12.4-11** and the Karl Rahner box (p. 19). The New Testament teaches that every Christian should exhibit *all* of the fruits of the Spirit, to some degree. But the *gifts* of the Spirit are spread around the body of Christ. Go round your group and help each member to identify one gift, which the Spirit has given them to be used 'for the common good'.

7. **Read Acts 2.1-4.** Some images of the Spirit in the Bible are strong and disturbing e.g. wind and fire. The worldwide Church in the 21st century is racked with strong disagreements and fiercely held opinions (e.g. female bishops, gay issues, celibacy ...). You might wish to discuss some of these – and the role of the Holy Spirit in showing the way forward.

8. A young person from your church asks you to explain or describe the Holy Spirit. What would you say?

9. **Read** the amusing box about the Bayeux Tapestry (p. 18). If invited, the Spirit of Jesus comes into our lives as a gentle power – *and* as a restless guest – wanting to make us more holy (he is the *Holy* Spirit!). Can you describe a time when the Spirit challenged you – perhaps to do or say something, or to re-order your priorities.

10. **Read 1 Corinthians 3.16-17.** Which areas of your lives – as individuals, as a group, as a church – need the Holy Spirit's power to disturb now?

11. Jim Wallis [track 41 on CD] suggests that we can't really follow Jesus without that extra 'something' which the Holy Spirit (*God's* Spirit) brings into our lives. What do you make of this assertion – and the statement by Harry Williams in the box on p. 18?

12. 'The Church will call for the use of power always in the light of the Cross which rightly has central place in every church' [track 42]. What does this mean in practice?

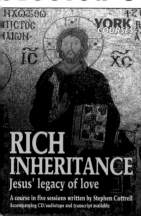

RICH INHERITANCE
Jesus' legacy of love
A course in five sessions written by Stephen Cottrell
Accompanying CD/audiotape and transcript available

A MEAL

The human mother will suckle her child with her own milk, but our beloved Mother, Jesus, feeds us with himself...

Mother Julian of Norwich

If angels could be jealous of men, they would be so for one reason: Holy Communion.

St Maximilian Kolbe

One beggar showing another beggar where he found bread.

D T Niles' definition of evangelism

As we celebrate the Eucharist ... we enter most profoundly into the vision of a world redeemed by the grace and mercy of God in Jesus; and we participate in the life-giving transformation of ourselves.

Dean Michael Sadgrove

I was recently asked what sustains me most in my walk with God. There are many things I could have said, but the first thing to spring into my mind was *Holy Communion*. It is the breaking and sharing of bread in remembrance of Jesus that most keeps me going in my Christian life. It is one of the things that Jesus gives to his Church, specifically when he asks – or instructs – his friends to 'do this in remembrance of me' (1 Corinthians 11.24). But what does that mean? And how is it that this most precious gift from Jesus is sometimes neglected in the Church today?

Time travel

Imagine that I'm taking you in a time machine. We travel back to Calvary on the Friday afternoon when Jesus was crucified. Imagine, too, that you don't know anything about the story. If I ask you what's happening, you'd probably say that a man is being executed. And at one level you'd be right. This is the most basic meaning of the cross. God in Jesus shares the awful, wretched suffering of the world. An innocent man goes humbly to a horrible death.

And if you knew a bit more about the Roman Empire, you would probably comment that crucifixions were two a penny. This was the way that thousands of criminals – and innocent people too – met their deaths.

Now imagine that I am bringing you back to the present day. We go to one of the great Christian cathedrals, where we witness a grand and splendid celebration of Holy Communion. If you know nothing about Christian worship, and if I ask you what's happening, you'd probably say that it's a sacrifice. There's an altar, a priest – so some sort of sacrificial ritual must be taking place. Again, what was happening would seem obvious.

But, of course, the Christian story in all its mysterious beauty is somewhat different. The death of Jesus that looks like an execution is actually the sacrifice. That man on the cross is God himself. He has come not just to *share* the sufferings of the world but to *redeem* them.

How did the first Christians ever reach these astounding conclusions?

- That it is death itself being strung up on the cross?
- That it is sin that is defeated?
- That this, the darkest hour, is really the brightest – the triumph of self-giving love?

Well, the first answer must be the resurrection. The raising of Jesus is the vindication of all that he stood for and all that he taught. But this still doesn't quite explain how they came to the idea that Jesus' death was a sacrifice. This is where the meal comes in ...

'This is my body broken for you ...'

I have already mentioned some of the strange and beguiling words that Jesus spoke on the night before he died. He washed his disciples' feet and left them the new commandment to 'love one another as I have loved you' (John 13). He told them that he had to go away so that the Spirit could come. Strangest of all, as he broke the bread at supper, he said, 'This is my body, broken for you' (1 Corinthians 11.23-26).

At the time they couldn't have understood what he meant. It would have seemed like one more riddle. But it all fell into place

- when they met him, risen from the dead
- when two disciples told their story of how, after their journey to Emmaus, Jesus was known to them in the breaking of bread

When they remembered that Last Supper in the light of the resurrection, they would have made the connection. Jesus had given them a way of interpreting what his death meant. His body broken on the cross was not just one more execution: it was his freely offered sacrifice for sin. In this respect the Last Supper is best understood as an acted parable – a story that illuminates the deep meaning of the cross and resurrection.

'Do this in remembrance of me'

The service of Holy Communion is sometimes called the *Eucharist*. This Greek word means 'thanksgiving'. For such it is – a solemn and joyful remembrance and thanksgiving for the passion, death and resurrection of the Lord Jesus himself. It is given to us as a way

- of *understanding* what his death means
- of *receiving* the fruits of his victory over sin and death for ourselves.

When Christians share Holy Communion today, we are not just passively remembering what Jesus did two thousand years ago. We are worshipping a living, risen ascended Lord. We are, in Archbishop David Hope's memorable phrase, 'remembering the future'. We are participating in the life of heaven – for the same Jesus who was known in the breaking of bread on the road to Emmaus, makes himself known to us today in the same way. This is why the bread of Holy Communion is sometimes called the 'bread of heaven'.

The meal of the Eucharist also contains within it all the things we have been exploring in this course:

- it is our remembrance of the Easter mystery
- it forms us as the people of God – re-telling the story of our salvation (for every service of Communion is a sharing of the Word, as well as of the bread)
- it is all done in and through the outpouring of the Holy Spirit.

This Service is indeed one of the great treasures of the Church. And until that day when we see the Lord face to face, it is one of the chief ways – and indeed, the way given by Jesus himself – for our covenant relationship with God to be renewed and sustained.

Eat here or take away?

One last thing. When you place your order in a fast food restaurant they often ask whether you want to eat here or take away. I believe God is asking us this same question today: these things that I have given you in Christ; these things that are brought together in the Eucharist, are you going to eat them here or take them away? *Are they just for you, or for sharing with the world?*

This is the vital question that every Christian and every Christian community must face: how are we going to respond to the great gifts that Jesus gives us? This rich inheritance; this legacy of love. And on this final note it is worth remembering that the word *'mass'* (the word that Catholic Christians often use to describe Holy Communion) has the same root as the word *'mission'*. They are both about being sent out with a take-away faith.

This then is our rich inheritance: an empty tomb, a group of people, a story, a power and a meal. This is Jesus' legacy of love. This legacy is given to his Church. But it is not for us alone. He calls us to share it with our hurting and divided world.

Older Anglicans will remember the days when Holy Communion was not the main Sunday Service. Then came the adage: 'The Lord's people around the Lord's table on the Lord's day'. Bishop F J Chavasse recollected the 'Communion Sundays' of his Victorian boyhood: 'My father would be extra quiet all day, and shut himself up in his room both before and after the service. I have seen him come down from the rail with tears in his eyes.'

QUESTIONS FOR GROUPS

BIBLE READING: 1 Corinthians 11.23-26

1. ***Read Luke 24.30-35.*** Describe a particularly memorable service of Holy Communion which you attended. In a special place, perhaps (a garden, a bedroom, a holy site ...) – or just an ordinary service which nonetheless felt 'special'.

2. Some Christians prefer simplicity: bread and wine on a table. Others like splendour: music, vestments, incense ... What are the strengths of each approach?

3. ***Read*** the box at foot of p. 23. In past generations – and in some churches today – Holy Communion was rare and therefore extra special. Have we lost something by making it so regular and frequent?

4. ***Read 1 Corinthians 11.27-34.*** Do you prepare yourself to receive Holy Communion? If so, how? When you receive the bread and the wine, what goes through your mind? How would you explain to an interested non-churchgoing friend what Holy Communion means to you?

5. All our participants agree that Holy Communion is 'very, very important to me' [43]. Archbishop Vincent adds [47], 'If you stand at the door of a church and you talk to people as they're leaving, they've been rejuvenated'. How would you respond to church-going friends who confide that they don't experience anything special or feel any different when they receive Holy Communion and who wonder if there's something wrong with them, spiritually.

6. In addition to Holy Communion, in what other ways are your relationship with Jesus sustained and strengthened? What part – if any – does church membership play in this for you?

7. Quakers and Salvationists don't break bread together in a special service. They maintain that *every* meal is a sacrament at which Jesus is present. How do you feel about this approach? Would it help

if modern Christians recaptured the old custom of saying Grace before we eat? American Christians often say Grace in restaurants. How do/would you feel about doing this?

8. ***Read Amos 5.21-24 & Romans 12.1-3*** Holy Communion often ends: 'Go in peace to love and serve the Lord.' We have been strengthened for service, so God sends us out ('apostles us') to be his ambassadors in word and deed. In one sense, our worship begins when we *leave* church. Do you feel the force of this?

9. ***Read 1 Peter 4.9 & Titus 1.8.*** When we invite someone for a meal, we think of *their* needs and preferences. 'Fresh expressions' is a movement within the churches which takes this seriously. Do you need to adapt your worship to encourage new people to join you, and to feel welcome and 'at home'?

10. ***Read John 14.1-3.*** Faith is a very personal thing – bringing comfort and challenge to countless lives. But a *purely* personal Christian faith is a contradiction in terms, for God calls us to *share* our good things. How might do you and your church share your 'take-away faith', with one another and in your locality? What are the barriers 'out there' in the world which might prevent people responding to our 'take away faith'?

11. The stress these days tends not to be on 'making my Communion' but on gathering around the Lord's table with the family of God. *Eucharist* means 'thanksgiving'. What difference does it make to your day-to-day life to be part of a community based on gratitude?

12. As this course comes to an end, you might want to plan ahead as a discussion group, a church or a group of churches.

13. Write down one thing you will take away from this course and share it with your group.